SPECTRUM®
READERS

LEVEL 3

W9-COW-293

STRANGE!
Plants

By Katharine Kenah

Carson-Dellosa
Publishing

SPECTRUM®

An imprint of Carson-Dellosa Publishing, LLC
P.O. Box 35665
Greensboro, NC 27425-5665

carsondellosa.com

The publisher would like to thank the NOAA Photo Library, NOAA
National Estuarine Research Reserve Collection; Waquoit Bay,
Massachusetts and Alison Robb for their permission to reproduce their
photograph used on page 12 of this publication.

01-002131120

Imagine a world without plants.
There would be no vegetables to eat.
There would be no wooden houses
to live in.
Without plants, there would be no
life on earth.

Plants are everywhere.
Some plants are big.
Some plants are small.
Some plants are weird and wacky!

Bird-of-Paradise

Is that a bird? No, it is a plant!
The bird-of-paradise is named after
its bright orange and blue flower.
The flower looks like the head of a bird.
This plant is native to South Africa.
A giant form of it grows in the state
of Hawaii in the United States.

Weird Facts

- Bird-of-paradise plants look like the flying birds-of-paradise, which are brightly colored birds.

- Seeds of the bird-of-paradise are poisonous if eaten.

6

Giant Water Lily

The largest water lily in the world
is the giant water lily.
Its round leaves are seven feet wide.
A person could lie down inside of one!
The giant water lily grows in the
warm waters of the Amazon River.
This river is in South America.

Weird Facts

- The giant water lily is also called the *Victoria amazonica.* It was named in 1838 after Queen Victoria of England.

- A giant water lily's flowers smell like butterscotch and pineapple.

Pitcher Plant

A pitcher plant is a death trap for bugs.
It smells sweet.
The red stripes make it look like meat.
A bug flies to the plant looking for a meal.
The inside is slippery and covered
with sharp hairs.
When a bug falls inside, it cannot get out.

Weird Facts

- Pitcher plants have a drug in them that makes bugs unsteady. Bugs wobble along the rims of the plants. Then, they fall down into these deadly traps.

- Pitcher plants have clear spots on them. Bugs fly toward these sunny "windows" to escape. But they crash into the leaf and fall into the belly of the plant.

Venus Flytrap

A fly lands on leaves that look like
an open mouth.
Snap! The leaves close.
The Venus flytrap has just trapped its food.
This plant has small hairs on its leaves.
The hairs sense when something is there.
The edges of the leaves lock to keep
bugs inside.

Weird Facts

- Venus flytraps snap shut in one-third of a second.
- It takes a Venus flytrap 8–20 days to eat a whole bug.

Poison Ivy

Do not touch these leaves.
They are poison ivy.
Poison ivy vines climb trees,
walls, and fences.
Poison ivy also forms into a bush.
Each leaf is made of three smaller leaves.
In spring, poison ivy leaves are red.
In summer, the leaves turn
shiny and green.

Weird Facts

- The leaves of poison ivy are poisonous all year long. Touching these leaves causes red, itchy bumps.

- An allergy to poison ivy is the most common one in the United States.

13

Saguaro Cactus

The saguaro is the largest cactus
in the United States.
It can grow to be 60 feet tall—
as tall as a six-story building.
A saguaro cactus grows in hot, dry deserts.
Its tall trunk and branches store water.
Sharp pins, called *spines*, cover
the saguaro cactus.

Weird Facts

- Some saguaro cacti are over 200 years old.
- Saguaro cacti can weigh ten tons—more than a school bus.

Foxglove

The foxglove gets its name from its flowers.
They are shaped like the fingers of a glove.
This purple plant looks pretty,
but it can cause harm.
A strong heart medicine is made
from foxglove leaves.
A small amount of this drug is good.
Too much of this drug can stop a heart!

Weird Facts

- Some tales say that fairies wore foxglove blossoms as gloves. Others say that foxes put them on their paws so that they could move quietly.

- All of the foxglove plant is poisonous if eaten.

17

Bamboo

Bamboo is giant grass with a strong stem.
Bamboo shoots grow close together
and very quickly.
Some grow three feet in one day!
Bamboo is used to make things,
like houses, shoes, fishing poles, rope,
and paper.

Weird Facts

- Layers of bamboo together are almost as strong as steel.
- Scientists think that bamboo is one of the world's earliest forms of grass.

Giant Sequoia

A giant sequoia is one of the biggest
and oldest living things on the earth.
It is a type of redwood tree.
The giant sequoia has a very large trunk.
Most trunks are 100 feet around.
It would take a circle of almost twenty
people holding hands to surround this
giant tree!

Weird Facts

- Giant sequoias live for thousands of years.

- The largest tree in the world is a sequoia
  called the *General Sherman Tree*. It is over
  274 feet tall and 102 feet around. It is almost
  five times taller than an adult oak tree.

Lichen

A lichen is a plant with no leaves,
roots, flowers, or stems.
It can live in the deep Arctic cold.
It can live in the hot desert heat.
It can live and grow on a rock!
A lichen is made of both algae and fungi.
Algae help the lichen make food.
Fungi hold water for the lichen.

Weird Facts

- Slow-growing lichens can live to be 4,000 years old.

- For 2,000 years, doctors have used drugs made from lichens to treat lung and skin problems.

Kelp

Kelp is a large brownish-green seaweed
that grows underwater.
It is found in cold waters around the world.
Many sea animals use kelp
for food or shelter.
Giant kelp grows very long
and very quickly.
It can grow over 300 feet in one year!

Weird Facts

- A lot of giant kelp living together forms
a kelp forest. There are no trees in
this forest, just kelp!

- Algin, made from kelp, is used to make ice
cream, paper, and toothpaste.

Cattail

Is that a cat hiding in the grass?
No, it is a cattail!
A cattail is a wild plant.
It lives along the edges
of ponds and lakes.
It has tall, pointy green leaves.
In the spring, a cattail has
a greenish-yellow flower.
By the end of summer, the flower is long,
dark, and fuzzy like a cat's tail.

Weird Facts

- Part of the cattail flower was once used to make silk. It is still used to make bandages for cuts.

- In some parts of the world, cattails are covered with oil and set on fire. They are used as lights.

27

Dandelion

A bright yellow dandelion
blooms all year long.
It opens during the day
and closes up at night.
A full-grown dandelion
has white, fluffy seeds.
The word *dandelion* means
"tooth of the lion."
People think the edges of its leaves look
like a row of lion's teeth.

Weird Facts

- The early colonists brought dandelion
  seeds to North America. They grew
  dandelions for food and medicine.

- Dandelions are edible weeds! They can be
  cooked or used in salads.

Orchid

Many gardeners think the orchid is
the most beautiful flower in the world.
It grows in every color except blue!
In warm places, an orchid will grow
in a tree.
In cool places, an orchid grows
on the ground.
Orchids are found in almost every type of
climate except deserts.

Weird Facts

- The vanilla vine is a climbing orchid. It
  produces pods called *vanilla beans*. The
  vanilla is used in drinks and foods.

- It takes some orchid plants up to four years
  to recover after producing a flower.

STRANGE! Plants
Comprehension Questions

1. Why are plants important?

2. Why do you think the bird-of-paradise was given its name?

3. Where might you find a giant water lily?

4. Why can bugs not get out of a pitcher plant after they fall inside?

5. What color are poison ivy leaves in the spring? What color are they in the summer?

6. What is the largest cactus in the United States? How tall can it grow?

7. How can the foxglove cause harm?

8. What is bamboo used for?

9. What is a lichen? Where can it be found?

10. What is kelp? How much can kelp grow in one year?

11. Why do you think the cattail was given its name?